Mastering Word for Novel Writing

Simplifying the Complex

Ben Taylor

Libromancy, LLC
PUBLISHING SERVICES

An Introduction

LET'S BE HONEST. For the novelist, Microsoft Word is often treated as a necessary evil. It's the sprawling, button-infested behemoth that came with our computers, a tool we tolerate more than we cherish. You wrestle your prose into it, you fight its bizarre formatting choices, and save your work with a quiet prayer that the whole teetering structure doesn't collapse under the weight of 100,000 words. You know, intuitively, that a program this powerful shouldn't be this frustrating.

And you are right.

This book was born from that very frustration. Its purpose is not to give you a guided tour of every tab, button, and drop-down menu Word has to offer. Frankly, nobody has time for that. The purpose of this book is to stop fighting with your word processor and start writing your novel. We are here to separate the signal from the noise, to identify the handful of tools that truly matter and to master them completely. This isn't about learning everything; it's about learning the right things.

So, who is this book for? It's for you. It's for the aspiring novelist who is rightfully intimidated by the program's sheer complexity. It's for the seasoned author who has published multiple books but is still haunted by the ghost of formatting-past, convinced there must be a more streamlined way to work. It's for any writer who has looked at their sprawling, unwieldy manuscript and thought, "There has to be a better way."

This book is my pledge to you that there is. By the end of our time together, you will have the skills to transform Word from an adversary into a powerful, reliable assistant.

You will learn to build a custom, bulletproof writing template that sets you up for success before you even type "Chapter One."

You will learn to navigate your manuscript with grace and speed, no matter how long or nuanced it becomes.

And you will learn to format your novel for editors, agents, and publication without wanting to throw your computer out a window.

Now, let's get to work.

A Writer's Five-Minute Tour of Word

ALRIGHT, fire up the program. The first thing you'll notice upon opening a new document is the sheer, unadulterated chaos of the interface. It's a bit like stepping into the cockpit of a 747 and being told to "just fly the plane." Buttons, tabs, and icons stretch across the horizon, each one silently judging you for not knowing its purpose.

This is by design. Word is made to serve everyone—the student, the scientist, the corporate drone, the legal secretary. But you are none of those things. You are a novelist, and your needs are far more specific.

The Illusion of Complexity

Let's quickly identify the main offenders on the screen. That monstrosity of options at the top is called the Ribbon. It's organized into tabs like Home, Insert, and Layout, and it is the source of most of our anxiety. It is a monument to the idea that more is always better, a notion that anyone who has ever tried to write a novel knows to be patently false. It's built for everyone, from the corporate drone to the legal secretary, which means it's not built particularly well for you, the novelist.

Our first move is one of glorious subtraction. We are going to make most of it disappear.

Look to the far right of the Ribbon, for a small upward-pointing caret (^). This unassuming little icon is your ticket to freedom. Click it. The Ribbon will collapse, tucking itself away and leaving you with nothing but the clean, elegant expanse of your page. If you don't see the caret (^) you can use Ctrl + F1 / Command + Option + R to toggle the Ribbon on and off.

Take a moment to appreciate it. The silence. The space. This is your new default view. You've just hidden ninety percent of the distractions.

"But what if I need one of those buttons?" you ask. Don't panic. The main tabs—Home, Insert, View, etc.—are still there. Simply click on one, and the Ribbon will glide gracefully back into view for you to select your command. Once you've done your business, click away, and it will vanish again. It's there when you need it, and gone when you don't. This isn't about abolishing the tools; it's about putting them in their proper place.

Setting the Stage

Now, for your first act of authorial intent. Go to File > New and select Blank document. You are now staring at a pristine, empty page. It is perfect. Let's immediately do the one thing that separates the professional from the amateur.

Let's save it properly.

We have all been there. A folder littered with files named MyNovel_Draft1.docx, MyNovel_v2_final.docx, and the inevitable, desperate MyNovel_final_final_USE_THIS_ONE.docx. This is not a filing system; it is a cry for help. A sane writer needs a sane system. From this day forward, I want you to use a simple, elegant convention: NovelTitle_YourName_YYYY-MM-DD.docx.

That's it. It's clean, it's chronological, and it will save you from a world of confusion. Find a folder for your project, save your new, blank document with today's date, and close it.

Congratulations. You've just imposed order on the chaos. That wasn't so hard, was it? Now we can get on with the real work of building your atelier.

The Unshakable Foundation

IF YOU ARE GOING to spend hundreds of hours in a single document, it ought to be a pleasant place to be. A writer's workspace is not merely functional; it's psychological. Before we type a single story-word, we must first build our digital atelier—a clean, stable, and personalized environment designed for the specific task of long-form narrative. This is where we stop being renters in Microsoft's world and become architects of our own.

The Aesthetics of Prose

First, let's address the look of the thing. The default settings in Word are designed for corporate memos, not for a novelist sinking into their fictional world. We can do better.

Your most immediate decision is the font. You will be staring at it for months, if not years. Do yourself a favor and choose something with serifs. Serif fonts—the ones with the little "feet" on the letters, like Times New Roman, Garamond, or Georgia—have been the standard for printed books for centuries for a simple reason: they are easier on the eyes over long reading sessions. Ditch the default Calibri or Arial. This is a novel, not an inter-office email. Pick something classic. Garamond is a personal favorite; it's elegant and has been carrying literature for half a millennium.

Next, give your words some room to breathe. The default single-spacing is cramped and intimidating. Adjust your line spacing to 1.5 or even double-spacing. This isn't for your final manuscript submission—we'll get to that later—this is for your comfort while you write and edit. Likewise, don't be afraid to go into the Layout tab and set generous margins. An inch and a half on all sides can make the page feel less crowded and more inviting.

The Non-Negotiable Keystone: Mastering Styles

Now for the main event. If you learn only one thing from this entire book, let it be this: You must use Styles.

I cannot overstate this. Using Styles is the single most important practice that separates a clean, manageable manuscript from a 400-page formatting nightmare. What is a Style? A Style is simply a named set of formatting rules. Instead of manually highlighting your chapter title and making it bold, 24-point, and centered every single time, you apply a Style called "Chapter Title."

"But that just saves a few clicks," you say. No. That is not what it does. It embeds structural information into your document. It tells Word, "This isn't just bold text; this is a chapter title." This distinction is everything.

Let's create the only two Styles you need to start. Find the Styles pane—it's usually on the Home tab.

You have now done more to ensure your manuscript's future stability than 90% of writers.

And now for the payoff. Go to the View tab and check the box for Navigation Pane. On the left side of your screen, a new panel will appear. Type "Chapter One" and apply your "Heading 1" Style to it. Now hit enter, and type a sentence of body text, which should automatically be in your "Normal" style. Now type "Chapter Two" on a new line and apply the "Heading 1" Style to it.

Look at your Navigation Pane. See those entries for "Chapter One" and "Chapter Two"? You've just created a clickable, interactive outline of your entire novel. As your book grows, this pane will become your map. You can jump between chapters instantly. You can even drag and drop them to restructure your entire novel on the fly. This is the power you unlock. It is not a trick; it is the reward for doing things the right way.

Your Master Blueprint: Creating the Perfect Novel Template

You have now perfected your writing environment. The fonts are pleasing, the spacing is comfortable, and the foundational Styles are in place. The last thing you want to do is repeat this process every time you start a new project. You won't have to.

We are going to save this work as a master blueprint. In Word, a normal document is a .docx file. A template, however, is a .dotx file. A template is a reusable mold. When you open it, it creates a new, untitled copy of itself, leaving the original blueprint untouched.

Here is how you forge your template:

That's it. From this day forward, when you want to start a new novel or short story, you will not open a blank document. You will go to File > New, and under your "Personal" templates, you will find "Novel Template." You will click it, and a brand new, perfectly configured manuscript will be born, ready for your words.

You have built your atelier. Now you are ready to work in it.

How to Organize a Beast of a Manuscript

A NOVEL IS A PECULIAR BEAST. It is, at once, a piece of art and a feat of engineering. The art is in the prose, the characters, the soul of the story. The engineering is in the structure—the scaffolding that holds the entire narrative up. A weak structure, no matter how beautiful the prose draped over it, will collapse. Fortunately, because we had the foresight to build our atelier on the bedrock of Styles, Word provides us with some surprisingly elegant tools for managing that structure.

The Macro View

Your first reward for using Styles was the Navigation Pane. It's your novel's table of contents, its interactive map. But sometimes, a map isn't enough. Sometimes you need to perform major surgery.

This is where Word's Outline View comes into play. Go to the View tab and click Outline.

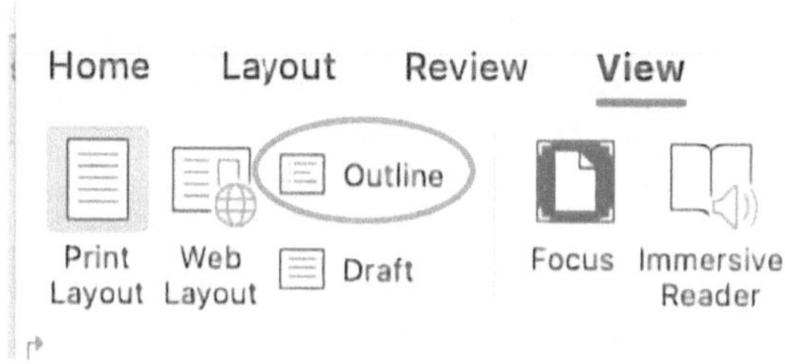

The world will change. Your manuscript will transform from a flowing river of text into a tiered, indented list. Every paragraph marked with your "Heading 1" Style will be a top-level item.

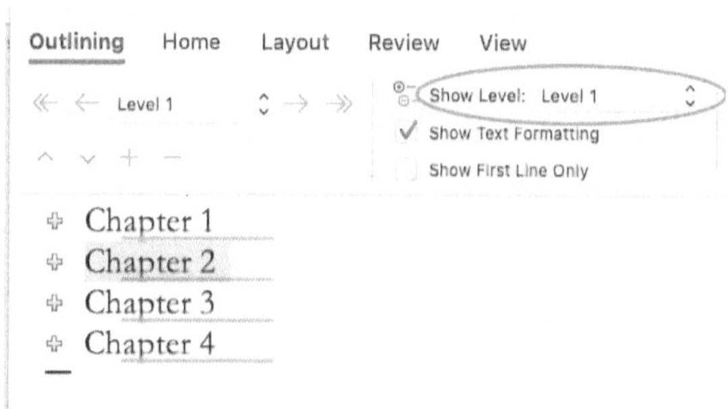

You can select Level 1 from the Show Level drop-down menu. This will collapse an entire chapter down to a single line, hiding the text within so you can see the grand sweep of your narrative. Want to move Chapter Seven to come before Chapter Six?

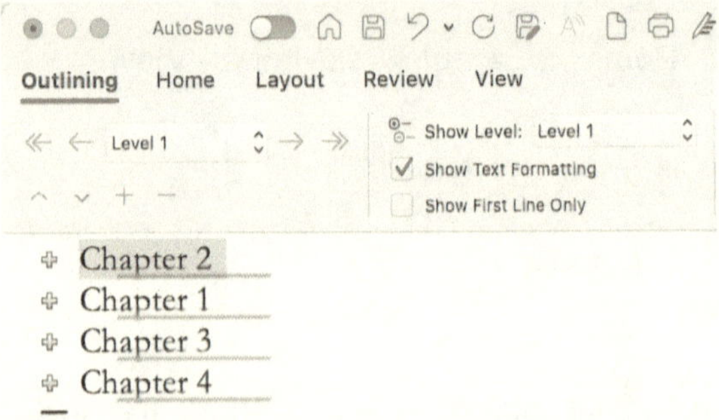

In the Outline View, you simply click the heading and drag it. The entire chapter—every word, every paragraph—moves with it. This is how you rearrange the skeleton of your story without the clumsy, error-prone nightmare of cutting and pasting thousands of words.

And now for the second payoff, the one that feels like genuine magic. Let's say you're ready to print your draft or send it to a beta reader. You need a table of contents. Find a blank page at the beginning of your document. Go to the References tab, click Table of Contents, and choose one of the automatic styles.

Poof.

A perfect, professionally formatted table of contents appears, complete with every chapter title and its corresponding page number. If you later add a chapter or move things around, you don't have to fix it manually. You just right-click on the table and select Update Field. Word does the work for you. This isn't a trick; it's the logical conclusion of the work we did setting up our Styles. You told Word what the chapter titles were, so Word knows how to build the map.

Bricks and Mortar

Now let's talk about the divisions between things. The amateur writer ends a chapter, hits the Enter key a dozen times to get to a new page, and calls it a day. This is a cardinal sin of manuscript formatting. It creates a fragile document where a single edit can cause a cascade of formatting disasters.

We will not do this. We will use the proper tools.

The simplest and most common tool is the Page Break. When you finish a chapter, instead of hitting Enter repeatedly, you insert a page break (Ctrl+Enter / Cmd+Enter or Insert > Page Break). This tells Word, "I don't care how much empty space is on this page; the next thing I type must start on a fresh page." It is clean, absolute, and stable. Every chapter should begin with one.

For more nuanced control, we have the Section Break. A section break is like a page break on steroids. It not only starts a new page but also creates an invisible wall in your document, allowing you to apply different formatting rules to each side of the wall. This is how you handle things like front matter. Your title page and copyright page shouldn't have page numbers, right? You place a section break after them, and you can then tell Word to start numbering on page one of Chapter One.

Speaking of which, let's demystify page numbering, a task that has driven countless writers to drink. Double-click in the footer area (the bottom margin) of your document to open the Header & Footer tools. Here, you can insert page numbers. But what about getting rid of the number on the first page of a chapter? While in the Header & Footer view, simply check the box that says Different First Page.

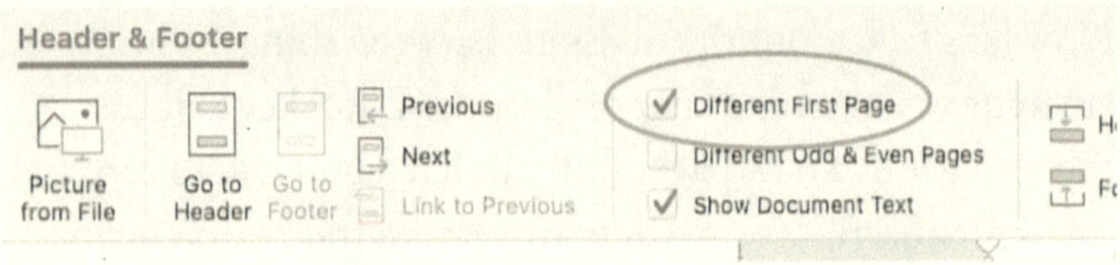

This gives you a separate, blank footer for the first page of every chapter (or every page in a new section), while the subsequent pages remain numbered.

This is the engineering. It isn't glamorous, but a well-placed break and a properly formatted page number are the literary equivalent of a level foundation and a plumb wall. They aren't the parts anyone will praise you for, but without them, the whole house falls down.

Editing Your Work Within Word

THERE IS a romantic notion that novels are born in a flurry of inspiration, the words flowing perfectly from mind to page. This is, to put it politely, a lie. First drafts are for getting the story down. The art happens in the revision. It is in the patient act of rewriting, cutting, and polishing that a messy draft is transformed into a novel. This is not a cleanup phase; it is the heart of the writing process itself. Word, for all its faults, offers a few remarkably sharp tools for this critical stage.

The Conversation with Yourself

Before you invite any other readers into your world, you must first become your own most thoughtful critic. This requires a way to step back from the text and comment on it, to have a dialogue with the writer you were yesterday.

This is the perfect job for Comments. While writing, you highlight a clunky sentence, an awkward piece of dialogue, or a plot point that feels weak. Go to the Review tab and click

New Comment. A small box will appear in the margin where you can leave a note for your future self. "Is this motivation believable?" "Find a stronger verb here." "This whole paragraph is telling, not showing." These comments become your revision roadmap, a to-do list for your next pass, allowing you to mark problems without interrupting your writing flow to fix them.

For more hands-on, experimental surgery, we have Track Changes. Most writers think of this as a tool for collaborating with an editor, and it is. But its true power is as a safety net for your own revisions. Turn on Track Changes from the Review tab. Now, every change you make—every deletion, every addition, every moved phrase—is recorded. Deleted text appears crossed out in red. New text appears underlined. You are free to tear your prose apart, to rewrite entire pages, to slash and burn with wild abandon, secure in the knowledge that no change is permanent until you "accept" it. It allows you to be ruthless, knowing that your original words are still there, just beneath the surface, if your bold experiment turns out to be a mistake.

But the real finesse, the granular control that elevated Track Changes from a simple on/off switch to a sophisticated editing tool, resided in the unassuming "Markup" dropdown menu. Located typically near the Track Changes button itself, this little menu offered a surprising degree of customization in how we viewed those recorded revisions.

Clicking it revealed a few key options. "Simple Markup" was often the default, providing a clean look with just a vertical line in the margin to indicate where changes had occurred. This was handy for getting a general sense of the edits without being overwhelmed by the visual cacophony of every strikethrough and underline.

However, for a deeper dive, we'd often select "All Markup." This unleashed the full visual record of our editing spree – the aforementioned red strikethroughs, the underlined additions, and even callout balloons in the margins detailing who made what change and when. It could look a bit like a digital Jackson Pollock painting, but it provided an undeniable level of detail. Then there were options like "No Markup," which temporarily hid all the tracked changes, allowing us to read the manuscript in its currently edited form without the distraction of the revisions. This was useful for assessing the flow and readability of the altered text.

Finally, "Original" displayed the document as it was before any tracking began, a comforting option when we needed a reminder of where we started. This level of control over the visual representation of our edits was invaluable. It allowed us to tailor our view depending on the stage of editing and the level of detail we needed to focus on, making the process far more manageable and less visually jarring than simply having all changes constantly and aggressively on display.

The Mechanical Eye

Once the larger structural and narrative issues are settled, you can turn your attention to the line-by-line mechanics. This is where you enlist some help, both from the machine and from your own discipline.

First, let's talk about the built-in Spelling & Grammar Check. You should use it. It is an unemotional, tireless proofreader that will catch a thousand tiny typos and spelling errors that your brain, which knows what a word is supposed to be, will glide right over. Run it, and humbly fix the obvious mistakes. However, you must treat its grammatical advice with deep suspicion. Word's grammar checker is a blunt instrument, and it has no understanding of voice, style, or rhythm. It will try to "fix" intentional fragments. It will question evocative but technically "improper" sentences. Listen to its spelling suggestions; largely ignore its creative writing advice.

The machine can only take you so far. The final backstop for consistency is you. For this, you must create a Style Sheet. This is not a feature in Word; it is a document you create for yourself. It can be a separate file or a few pages at the end of your manuscript. Here, you will be the ultimate authority. You will record every important, specific detail:

A style sheet is a simple, powerful tool that ensures the color of your protagonist's eyes doesn't change in Chapter Fifteen. It's the final, human touch of professionalism that no automated checker can ever replicate.

Tools for Writing and Research

THE GRAND ARCHITECTURE of your novel is set. The foundation is stable, the sections are framed out, and you have a map to navigate the whole affair. Now comes the real work: filling that structure with words, day after day. This is the daily grind, the process of laying one brick at a time. While much of this is pure creative effort, Word has a few tools that can make the labor less arduous and your process more organized.

The Art of Dialogue

Dialogue is the lifeblood of most novels, and formatting it correctly is a non-negotiable mark of professionalism. The basic rules are simple enough: punctuation generally goes inside the quotation marks, and a new speaker gets a new paragraph.

But we can be more thoughtful than that. Just as we created Styles for our body text and headings, we can create one for dialogue. Why bother? Imagine you are 60,000 words into your manuscript and decide that you want all your dialogue paragraphs to have a slight hanging indent to distinguish them more clearly from the narration. Are you going to go back and change thousands of paragraphs by hand? Of course not.

Instead, you can create a new Style called "Dialogue." Base it on your "Normal" Style, so it inherits the same font and size. The only change you might make, for now, is to ensure it has the same spacing as your narrative text. You apply this Style to every paragraph of spoken word. Later, if you want to change the look of all your dialogue, you modify the Style once, and the entire manuscript updates instantly. It's about working smarter, not harder.

Finding Your Place

A novel is a sprawling country, and it's easy to get lost in it. You might be writing a scene in Chapter Twenty and suddenly need to recall the exact wording of a promise a character made back in Chapter Two. Scrolling endlessly is for amateurs.

This is a job for Bookmarks. A Bookmark in Word is exactly what it sounds like: an invisible marker that you can name and jump to at any time. Highlight a key phrase, a character's introduction, or a sentence you need to fact-check later. Go to the Insert tab and click Bookmark. Give it a short, memorable name (like Annas Promise or Gun In Desk) and click Add. The marker is now set.

To find it again, you can use the power-user's secret weapon: the "Go To" command. Press Ctrl+G / Cmd + Option + G to bring up the "Go To" dialog box. From here, you can instantly jump to a page number, a section, a heading, or, most usefully, a named bookmark. It's your manuscript's teleportation device. Once you get in the habit of bookmarking key moments as you write them, you'll never waste time scrolling again.

Keeping Your Notes Close

A novel rarely springs fully formed from the imagination. It is supported by a scaffolding of research, notes, and half-forgotten ideas. While some writers prefer a separate notebook or application for this, you can keep essential notes tethered directly to the text.

We've already discussed using Comments for editing, but for research, Footnotes can be surprisingly useful. Don't think of them in the academic sense. Think of them as a private note to yourself. Did you just invent a street name? Drop a footnote and write, "Check if a 'Maple Drive' exists in 1950s Cleveland." Did a character mention their eye color? Footnote it: "Hazel eyes. Remember this." These notes stay anchored to the relevant text but live at the bottom of the page, out of the way of your creative flow. When you're done, you can delete them all.

For external resources—a Google Map of your setting, a web page on vintage firearms, a Pinterest board of character inspiration—you can embed hyperlinks. Highlight a relevant word (his Colt revolver), press Ctrl+K / Cmd+K, and paste the web address. The link is now part of your document, a quick click away, saving you from toggling between windows and losing your train of thought.

These are the small habits that keep a large project from descending into chaos. They are the tidy workshop of a master craftsman.

Preparing for Publication

FOR MONTHS, perhaps years, your novel has been a private world, a conversation between you and your characters. Now, that is about to change. The moment comes when the manuscript must leave the nest, to be seen by other eyes—agents, editors, beta readers, and eventually, the public. This transition from a personal project to a professional product is a critical one, demanding a new kind of rigor. It is time to put on a different hat, to move from artist to artisan, and to prepare your work for the marketplace.

The Editor's Dance: Collaborating with Others

Sharing your work is an act of vulnerability. Sharing your work with an editor who will proceed to bleed all over it in red ink is an act of professional courage. The tools we used for self-revision, Track Changes and Comments, now become the language of this collaboration.

When you receive an edited manuscript, it will likely be a sea of red and a flurry of comments in the margins. Your first job is to not panic or become defensive. This is the process. The editor is your partner, not your adversary. Use the Review tab to navigate the changes. You can move from one edit to the next, and for each suggestion, you have a choice: Accept or Reject. Accepting the change makes it a permanent part of the text. Rejecting it dismisses the suggestion.

The comments are where the real conversation happens. An editor might not just fix a sentence but explain why it was weak. Read these comments. Process them. If you agree, make the change and then right-click the comment and delete it. If you disagree or need clarification, use the Reply function to respond. This creates a clean, threaded conversation, a record of your decisions. This dance of feedback and revision is how a good book becomes a great one.

The Great Divide: Formatting for Digital vs. Print

The final manuscript is not a single, one-size-fits-all entity. The file you prepare for a Kindle ebook is fundamentally different from the one you prepare for a paperback. This is the great divide, and understanding it will save you untold grief.

First, The Ebook Tango. The beauty of an ebook is its reflowable text; the reader can change the font size and style. The consequence is that much of your beautiful, specific formatting will be stripped away. This is why our foundational work with Styles is so critical. Ebook conversion software doesn't care about your font choice; it cares about the structure. It sees your "Heading 1" Style and knows, "This is a chapter title." It sees your "Normal" Style and knows, "This is body text." A manuscript built correctly with Styles will convert cleanly into an EPUB file with a navigable table of contents. A manuscript formatted manually with tabs and spaces will become a garbled mess.

Second, The Printed Page. Print is a different beast entirely. Here, the layout is fixed, and every detail matters. This is the world of typesetting, and while professional designers handle the final version, you can prepare your manuscript for them. You must now become aware of "widows"—a single, lonely word at the end of a paragraph—and "orphans"—a single line of a paragraph stranded at the top of a new page. You can fix these by making minor edits to the text to shorten or lengthen a paragraph by a single line. You can also control where chapters begin, using Section Breaks to ensure that chapters starts on an Odd Page (a "recto" in publishing parlance), as is the convention.

The Final Step

Before you attach that file to an email, there are a few final acts of professional courtesy.

When submitting to an agent or publisher, you will almost always send a PDF. Why? Because a PDF is a snapshot. It locks your formatting in place. It guarantees that what they see on their screen is exactly what you see on yours, regardless of their version of Word or their computer's default fonts. Go to File > Save As and create a PDF. It is the professional standard.

Be mindful of the requested file format. While PDF is common for submissions, an editor you are working with will require the .docx file so they can use Track Changes. Some online submission forms may even ask for a .txt file, which strips away all formatting. Read the submission guidelines and give them exactly what they ask for.

Finally, and this is the most important advice in this entire chapter: Back up your novel. A hard drive crash is not a question of if, but when. Relying on a single file on your laptop is professional malpractice. Embrace the 3-2-1 rule: at least three copies of your data, on two different types of media (e.g., your computer and an external hard drive), with at least one copy located off-site (e.g., a cloud service like Dropbox, Google Drive, or OneDrive). Your novel is the culmination of countless hours of your life. Protect it as such.

Troubleshooting & FAQs

SOONER OR LATER, it happens. Despite your best efforts, your careful planning, and your professional habits, Word will do something utterly baffling. A paragraph will refuse to align, page numbers will embark on a journey of their own, or the program will grind to a halt. It's the nature of any complex tool. The goal is not to prevent every problem—that's impossible—but to know how to diagnose and solve the common ones without panicking. Think of this chapter as your calm, collected emergency contact.

Common Formatting Gremlins and Their Extermination

Your manuscript is haunted. A specific paragraph has a bizarre indent you can't get rid of, or a huge, unexplainable white space has appeared between chapters. Before you do anything drastic, it's time to turn on the lights and see the ghosts.

On the Home tab of the Ribbon is a peculiar little symbol that looks like a paragraph mark (¶).

This is the "Show/Hide ¶" button. Click it. Your document will suddenly be filled with little blue dots (spaces), arrows (tabs), and ¶ marks (paragraph breaks). This is Word's secret language. This view shows you the invisible architecture of your page. You can now see if that weird spacing is caused by someone hitting the Enter key ten times instead of inserting a proper page break. You can see if that odd indent is from a stray tab character. This is your primary diagnostic tool.

You can go through fixing each problem, but if a section of text is truly possessed by formatting demons, it may be time for an exorcism. This is the "Clear All Formatting" button, located on the Home tab (it looks like an 'A' with an eraser).

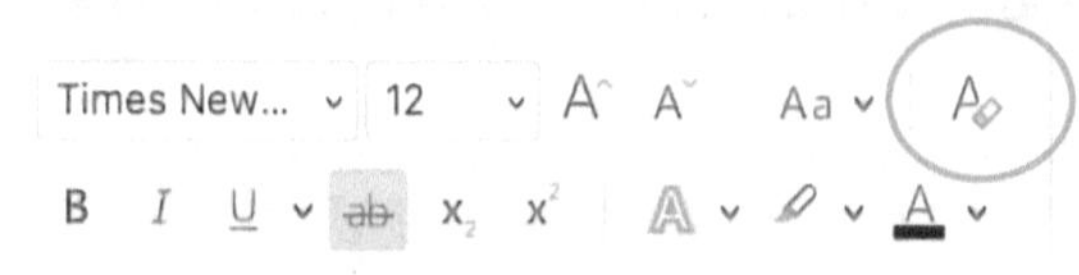

Highlight the misbehaving text and click this button. It is the nuclear option. It will strip away all local formatting and revert the text to your basic "Normal" Style. From there, you can reapply the correct Style you intended to use in the first place.

And what about the ultimate disaster—a crash, a power outage, an accidentally closed file? Before you despair, check Word's recovery systems. The next time you open the program after a crash, it should automatically present you with an AutoRecover pane showing any available recovered files. If it doesn't, you can go to File > Info > Manage Document > Recover Unsaved Documents. It's not a perfect system, but it has saved many a chapter from the digital void.

Questions from the Trenches

Over the years, I've heard the same panicked questions from writers wrestling with their manuscripts. Here are a few of the most common.

"Why does my formatting get destroyed when I paste text from the internet?"

Because you are not just pasting text; you are pasting all the invisible, messy web formatting that comes with it. When you paste (Ctrl+Alt+V / Cmd+Option+V), you will see options, but "Unformatted Text" (the safest option). "Unformatted Text" strips out everything but the pure words, allowing you to apply your own clean Styles. Make it a habit.

"My page numbers are completely wrong. How do I restart the numbering for my main story?"

This is almost certainly a Section Break issue. Remember from Chapter IV: your document is not one continuous scroll. To restart page numbering, you need to create a wall between your front matter (title page, etc.) and your main text. Insert a Section Break (Next Page) after your front matter. Now, you can go into the header of your first chapter, unlink it from the previous section (uncheck the

"Continue from previous section" button), and set the page number to start at 1.

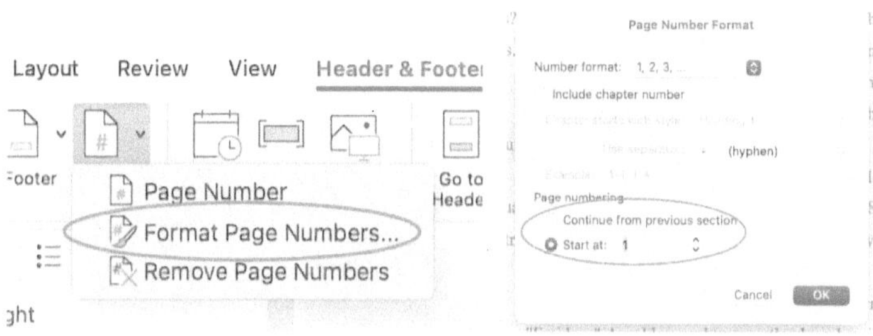

"My novel is 150,000 words long, and Word is running incredibly slow. What can I do?"

You are trying to maneuver a cargo ship in a bathtub. A single file of that size will tax the program. You can try working in "Draft" view (from the View tab), which hides complex formatting and images, speeding things up considerably. The more robust solution, however, may be to break the manuscript into more manageable parts—perhaps three separate files for "Part 1," "Part 2," and "Part 3." You can work on them individually and combine them into a master document only when you need to finalize the entire book.

Wrapping It Up

AND SO, we arrive at the end of our work together. We began with a simple, almost radical premise: that Microsoft Word, a program notorious for its complexity, could be honed into a simple, elegant, and powerful tool for the specific art of writing a novel. The goal was never to learn the function of every last button. The goal was to make the tool disappear, to build a workspace so clean and reliable that you could forget about the software and focus entirely on the story you are trying to tell. If we have succeeded, the program is no longer an obstacle between your idea and the page. It is a quiet, competent servant.

What We Have Built

Let's take a moment to look back at the ground we've covered. We did not learn Word; we tamed it.

We took a cluttered, chaotic interface and carved out a serene space. We traded the brute force of manual formatting for the intelligent structure of Styles, the single most important concept in manuscript management. We used that foundation to build an interactive map of our novel, to create an automated table of contents, and to ensure our work would convert cleanly for any digital platform. We established professional habits for organizing, revising, and collaborating.

Most importantly, we built a master template—a perfect, reusable blueprint for every story to come. You are no longer starting from scratch. You are starting from a position of control, with a system designed for the specific rigors of long-form fiction.

Onward, Writer

Now, you must forget all of this.

Not the habits, of course. They should become second nature. But you must now let the technical fade into the background. A carpenter who has mastered his tools does not think about the hammer; he thinks about the house he is building. Your task was never to become a Word expert. Your task is to be a writer.

The journey of writing a novel is long, arduous, and often lonely. It is a challenge of spirit and imagination, not of software proficiency. There is no tool or technique that can give you the perfect character, the unforgettable line of dialogue, or the ending that satisfies the soul. That work remains yours and yours alone.

All we have done here is clear the path. We have removed the technical rocks and roots that might trip you up along the way. The rest of the journey is up to you. Trust your story, be patient with your process, and write the book that only you can write.

The Wider World

This book was intentionally narrow, focused on a single tool for a single purpose. But the world of writing is vast. Should you wish to continue learning, there are endless resources available.

If you want to refine your storytelling technique, you might explore workshops such as those offered by the Gotham Writers Workshop or join online communities like Critique Circle, where writers exchange feedback and support. Those eager to master the art of revision can study books like "Self-Editing for Fiction Writers" by Renni Browne and Dave King, or "On Writing: A Memoir of the Craft" by Stephen King, both rich with practical exercises and insights.

Delving deeper into the craft, you might listen to podcasts such as "Writing Excuses" or "The Creative Penn," which bring together the collective wisdom of experienced authors. For genre-specific advice, resources like "Save the Cat! Writes a Novel" for plotting, or "The Emotional Craft of Fiction" by Donald Maass for deepening character, offer targeted guidance.

If you wish to polish your technical skills, online guides and video tutorials for Scrivener, Vellum, or other writing software can help you explore new tools.

Beyond books and courses, local writing groups, literary festivals, and open-mic nights can help you find your tribe, share your work, and grow in confidence. The world beyond these pages is brimming with opportunity.

Whatever direction you choose—be it through formal education, peer-to-peer critique, or solo experimentation—remember: every writer's path is unique. Explore widely, experiment boldly, and shape a creative journey that is entirely your own.

Our work here is done. Go build your world.

Appendices

THE LESSONS ARE OVER, but the work is just beginning. What follows is not another chapter to be read, but a toolkit to be used. These are the cheat sheets, the glossaries, and the blueprints you can refer to in the heat of the moment when you need an answer quickly. Keep this section handy.

Appendix A: Glossary of Terms

A brief dictionary of the jargon we've used, translated into plain English.

Bookmark: An invisible marker you can place in your text to quickly navigate back to a specific spot. Your manuscript's internal GPS.

Orphan: A single line of a paragraph stranded by itself at the top of a new page. A sad, lonely thing that should be fixed by minor text edits.

Page Break: A command that forces all subsequent text to start on a new page. The professional way to end a chapter.

PDF (Portable Document Format): A file format that creates a perfect snapshot of your document, locking the formatting in place. The standard for submitting your work.

Quick Access Toolbar: The small, customizable toolbar at the very top-left of the Word window.

Ribbon, The: The sprawling, tab-based menu system at the top of Word that contains every command and function. We have learned to master parts of it and, more importantly, to ignore the rest.

Section Break: A powerful command that creates a wall within your document, allowing different sections (like your front matter and your main chapters) to have entirely different formatting, such as page numbering.

Style: The absolute keystone of good manuscript formatting. A named, pre-defined set of formatting rules (for font, size, spacing, etc.) that you can apply to text. Using Styles is what makes your document structured, not just decorated.

Template (.dotx): A master blueprint of a document. When you open a template, it creates a new, untitled copy with all your preferred settings and Styles already in place.

Track Changes: The editing feature that records every addition, deletion, and change made to a document. Essential for collaborating with an editor and for safely revising your own work.

Widow: A single word or very short phrase stranded by itself on the last line of a paragraph. The close cousin of the orphan, and just as undesirable in professional typesetting.

Appendix B: Quick Reference Guide

For when you need the right command, right now. Shortcuts are listed in a Windows / macOS format.

Essential Word Shortcuts: Windows & Mac

Action	Windows Shortcut	Mac Shortcut
Save	Ctrl + S	Cmd + S
Save As	F12	Cmd + Shift + S
Show/Hide Formatting (¶)	Ctrl + Shift + 8	Cmd + 8
Insert Page Break	Ctrl + Enter	Cmd + Return
Insert New Comment	Ctrl + Alt + M	Cmd + Option + M
Go To (Page, Bookmark, etc.)	Ctrl + G	Cmd + Option + G
Find	Ctrl + F	Cmd + F
Apply "Normal" Style	Ctrl + Shift + N	Cmd + Shift + N
Apply "Heading 1" Style	Ctrl + Alt + 1	Cmd + Option + 1
Paste as Plain Text	Ctrl + Alt + V	Cmd + Option + Shift + V
Turn Track Changes On/Off	Ctrl + Shift + E	Cmd + Shift + E
Insert Footnote	Ctrl + Alt + F	Cmd + Option + F

↓

Appendix C: Sample Novel Template

Here is the blueprint for the template we built, a checklist of the essential elements it should contain. When you create your "Novel Template," ensure it has these features pre-configured.

Page Setup:

Paper Size: 8.5" x 11" (US Letter)

Margins: 1.25" on all sides (or your personal preference)

Pre-defined Styles:

Normal: The style for your main body text.

Font: Garamond (or your personal preference), 12 pt.

Alignment: Left

Line Spacing: 1.5 lines

Indentation: First line indented by 0.5"

Heading 1: The style for all chapter titles.

Font: Garamond (or your personal preference), 16 pt., Bold

Alignment: Center

Spacing: 24 pt. space before the paragraph

Header & Footer Settings:

Header: Configured to show Author Name / Book Title / Page Number in the top-right corner.

Page Numbering: Set to begin after the front matter (requires a Section Break).

Options: The "Different First Page" box is checked, ensuring no header or page number appears on the first page of a new chapter.

About the Author

Ben Taylor has been a trusted guide in the world of IT for over two decades. With a career dedicated to helping everyday computer users navigate the complex and often confusing world of technology, Ben has a knack for breaking down intricate concepts into straightforward, relatable advice. His passion for demystifying computers and making them accessible to everyone has made him a go-to resource for those looking to embrace the digital age with confidence.

Beyond his technical expertise, Ben is also an accomplished author of mysteries and thrillers, bringing the same analytical precision that serves him in IT to crafting suspenseful narratives that keep readers on the edge of their seats. When he's not troubleshooting, teaching, or penning his next page-turner, Ben enjoys exploring new tech trends and writing guides that simplify the ever-evolving landscape of IT.

www.gbtaylor.com

www.ingramcontent.com/pod-product-compliance
Lightning Source LLC
LaVergne TN
LVHW090433210926
848480LV00002B/817

* 9 7 9 8 2 3 1 0 6 3 1 9 2 *